Journey of a Visionary

"But they that wait upon the LORD shall renew their strength; they shall mount up with wings as eagles; they shall run, and not be weary; and they shall walk, and not faint." Isaiah 40:31

Patricia Esther Secke

Journey of a Visionary

By

Patricia Esther Secke

Copyright © 2011 Patricia Secke

ISBN

978-2-9539304-2-9

EAN

9782953930429

A few names have been changed in order to protect identities. All quotations are from the authorized Louis Second version bible.

This book has been translated from the French by Melyanne Mbuyi.

Contact Email:
patricia.secke@outlook.com

ACKNOWLEDGMENTS

I thank the Lord Jesus who has directed my life and has chosen me as a worker in His harvest.

I thank all those who have supported me in my afflictions, in my times of distress, as well as those who believed in me.

I sincerely want to thank Mrs. Aurelia Mendes Talamaku, Mrs. Mado Delcazi, Mrs. Nona Chili, Mrs. Rose Lukano and Mrs. Jacqueline Kelle for their precious support.

I would like to say thank you to all the pastors who have taught me the Word of God since the beginning of my conversion, and who have contributed in giving me solid food in my spiritual ascension since 2007 to this date.

A special thank you to Pastor Elie kiti, Pastor Jean Paul Munganga, Pastor Nestor Kamuanga, Reverend Charles Talingano, the Watchmen in Washington D.C and the pastoral couple Esther and Moussa Touré for their support and prayers.

Patricia Esther Secke

DEDICATION

This book is dedicated with great affection to my husband, Dr. Leopold Secke, who with love and tenderness supports me in my mission. His encouragements in difficult times comforted me greatly. I thank the Lord for selecting for me a man who gives me his full attention.

PREFACE

In recent years, the leading of the Holy Spirit has been one of the biblical truths which interests me the most. All those who wish to get acquainted with the leading of the Holy Spirit will certainly benefit from the book of our sister Patricia, which ministry consists in promoting women's talents and encourage them to work in unity to impact the world.

Despite a solid training as a Marketing and Business Strategy Engineer, and appropriate and useful connections, the beginnings of the ministry remained modest and sometimes bleak especially when it came to financial "fiasco".

It was during those years that we see "Patricia" showing great faith in face of adversity and a determination to pursue the vision embedded in her by the working of the Holy Spirit.

Having successfully passed the basic classes of faith, Patricia was able to enter in the dimension of the leading of the Holy Spirit who taught her the golden lesson: "The word of God is the solution to all problems; when it is meditated, pressed with faith, it

Patricia Esther Secke

produces a special anointing and operates the miracle because it cannot return to God void".

The publication of "Journey of a Visionary" gives the opportunity to many of us to discover the walk of a woman with Christ.

Reverend Dr. MOUSSA TOURE

Senior pastor, Bethel World Outreach Capitol Church, Washington D.C

CONTENTS

Patricia Esther Secke

Journey of a Visionary

Patricia Esther Secke

INTRODUCTION

On December 16, 2008, I made the commitment to open myself to the leading of the Holy Spirit, to surrender everything to Him and to wait for his answer.

I came to understand when making this decision, that in order to fulfill my mission on this earth, walking with Jesus was paramount. Not walking with Jesus in mere words but walking with Jesus with all my heart; that is to follow his instructions: through the Holy Scriptures and the leading of his Spirit. Our wonderful Lord didn't hide anything from us and recommended us to walk by his Spirit as stated in the 16th chapter and 13rd verse of the book of John: "When the comforter is come, the Spirit of truth, he will guide you into all truth; because he will not speak of himself but he will tell you everything that he has heard, and he will show you things to come".

I was able by this revelation to come out of religion, fear, and worry. Then the peace of God, which passes all understanding, filled me. This peace keeps my heart and my thoughts in Christ Jesus. I discovered my true nature; the nature of a King's child, the daughter of God who trusts her father.

I realized the abundant grace of the Lord on my life. Why did he decide to choose me for such a great mission? I wasn't better than anyone else, if not for the grace. I am not smarter than anyone else; it is only through the power of God and for his glory.

This awareness of this grace on my life has comforted me in my walk with Christ. I now know one thing which is that I will accomplish my mission provided I keep my eyes focused on Jesus, by consulting him and him alone; given that the revelation of Jesus is the engine of the fulfillment of my vision on this earth. Galatians 1 verse 15: " But when it pleased God, who separated me from my mother's womb, and called me by his grace, to reveal his Son in me, that I might preach him among the heathen; immediately I conferred not with flesh and blood: "

On December 16, 2008, I was in Washington, DC in the United States, where I had gone two months prior for the preparations of the 3rd International Congress of Black Women to be held in the Democratic Republic of Congo in Kinshasa. A mission the Lord entrusted me towards the end of 2006 in a dream. I have been working for the promotion of women's talents since 2003. My first experience was in Cameroon in 2004 where I organized an event for women, in order to promote their talents: "The Palms for the Excellence of women", an event highlighting the accomplishments of the woman who carries out projects with limited means. The same year, a record setting Congress of the Black Women Leader was held in Paris at the UNESCO, organized by the french-martiniquese Sandra Monthieux Pelage.

Following the first edition of "the Palms for the Excellence of Women" in Douala, Cameroon, I got in touch with Sandra Monthieux Pelage, then living in Houston in the United States and I in Paris. She had undertaken the organization of a second Congress of the Black Woman Leader in Houston in 2005, and we agreed to work together for the success of this initiative.

I was in charge of the promotion of the Convention in Africa and Europe, and I led a delegation of about 20 people. Following a total failure, our beautiful project was stopped. Approximately forty people in total accounted for the audience, in a room reserved for two thousand people.

I continued to work for the promotion of the talents of women in Africa. In 2006, God revealed himself to me and commanded me to pursue this mission, to keep bringing black women together not only in Africa but around the world for a purpose I didn't know at the time. Knowing human nature, my fear was that Sandra would claim to be the first to have come up with this concept of bringing black women together. But soon enough, by conducting some research in this area, I discovered that Dr. Dorothy. I. Height was the first to organize the gathering of black women, in 1935 in the United States.

After making this discovery, I had the assurance Sandra would come back one day to work alongside me. I do not know where she currently is, but my prayer is to see her again so that together we may resume the substantive work we started.

Right after committing to follow the leading of the Holy Spirit on December 16, 2008, I entrusted him the situation I faced, seeking his direction: unemployed, and without any money, I was wondering if I should find a job and work on the mission after putting some money aside?

I had already organized two major women's conferences and I had accumulated a lot of debts. Should I get a job and wait for a better time to continue?

Three days later, I had to return to Paris for two months. Being in a precarious financial situation, I asked the Holy Spirit if his will was for me to find a job once in Paris in order to pay for my living expenses and pay back the numerous debts closing in on me. I was expecting an answer.

On December 19, 2008, I boarded on a Northwest Airlines plane, to Paris via Amsterdam. At 17:35 pm, turbulence began to shake the plane and I started to intercede and pray in the spirit (in tongues). Right at this moment, I received the answer I was expecting. The answer to the question I asked the

Holy Spirit three days before the trip. It was clear: "write and testify of my kindness towards you, make my people know my great works and your salary will ensue". I received the confirmation of this revelation in the Holy Scriptures which says: "Drink waters out of thine own cistern and running waters out of thine own well" Proverbs 5, verse 15.

By presenting you the beginning of the journey of my vision, my aim is to encourage many visionaries gestating. The world in which we live is in need of visionaries. Africa needs visionaries, women need visionaries, and young people need role models in society to aspire to something.

Let the flow of the grace of God run over your lives. Give yourself totally to his spirit. Open your heart to him, unlock your destiny and impact your generation in the name of Jesus Christ our Lord.

Chapter 1

MY STEPS TOWARDS MY MISSION

Chapter 1: MY STEPS TOWARDS MY MISSION

My biography

I was born in a Cameroonian family. In 1992, I left Cameroon after my Baccalaureate in liberal arts for France to pursue my education. My mother wanted me to specialize in interpretation seeing that I have an aunt who had this trade and was making a good living. To please my mother, I registered at the Faculty of letters and Human Sciences in Nantes, in applied foreign languages.

I didn't have any passion for this curriculum, and I confess I was an average student who was rather drawn by studies on Leadership and International Relations. After two years, without telling my mother, I transferred to a business school, for a major in Marketing and Business Strategies.

In 1999, I got my engineering degree in Marketing and Business Strategies at the European Higher Institute of Management of Paris. I was happy, ready to find the best employment and fulfill my professional dreams: working in a multinational or becoming a Marketing Director for a large company in France. However, my dreams quickly faded as the reality was quite different from what I had anticipated.

My Setbacks

I launched myself into a job search for two years without any results. The job search was not easy. I experienced discrimination, and rejection. I spent sleepless nights on the internet looking for employment, sending out résumés to companies by mail, by fax, through temp agencies. A few times I received phone calls in the morning for conclusive appointments for job interviews; only, when I came in person to sign the contract, my color did not match the criteria for selection of these French companies.

My dream of working in a multinational company started to dim and I began to seriously worry. Two years passed, I stopped receiving financial assistance from my parents and I had just turned 31 years old.

A graduate, unemployed, with unpaid rents and many frustrations, I met by the grace of God my first husband, Roger Faraut. A few months later we got married, in June 2002. I had a resurgence of hope, and I thought my frustrations and problems were over. But very quickly, I was disillusioned when he asked me to share all the household expenses. The frustration of unemployment persisted, and I had, in order to be financially free to take the first job offer presented to me. It was done without the employer mentioning that he would not pay me at my fair value considering my level of education and the high quality of my diploma.

Consequently, I had to downgrade my resume, remove my Marketing Engineer courses, and only mention the Baccalaureate degree obtained in Douala and the two years spent at the University of Nantes. I was therefore hired in a travel agency which organized cruises around the world. I was of course only good enough to receive all calls and distribute the mail to the executives of the various departments.

After two months, the Assistant to the Director of Marketing was transferred to Toulon in the South of the France. I thought it was a great opportunity for me to apply for this internal position. I took the resolution to meet the Assistant to the president to tell her I was a graduate of the ISEG Paris, and I had lowered my skill level for economic reasons. I had nothing to lose anyway; on the other hand, I had a Marketing Assistant position to gain. As they say: "Nothing ventured, nothing gained" with the appointment set, and my real resume (including my academic curriculum and my diploma of the ISEG in Paris) in hand, I spoke with the manager who initially seemed nice and understanding.

After my presentation, she told me she would speak to the boss. Unfortunately, I never received any answer except for a silent pressure she exerted on me. I was kindly let go from the travel agency three weeks later. The counselor at the temp agency who had hired me told me this Assistant to the Director-General got the internal position because of her seniority. She went from Marketing Assistant to General Management Assistant. She had no diploma and to maintain her position, the only thing she had to do was to get rid of me quickly. It was done after three weeks.

We were already in 2003. Tired, I was wondering what I was going to do. I really wanted to be independent. I wanted to achieve things, to serve. Then, I had the idea of creating a company. I had the method, since I learned it in business school. I thought it would be child's play, but very soon again, the reality on the ground was different.

My grandfather was a cook, my mother is the owner of a restaurant in Cameroon (one of the best restaurants of the economic capital), and my brother is also a cook, a graduate of the catering school on the island of Noirmoutier in France. Why not create a new concept of fine African restoration in the Paris area?

I thought I had a plan that would bring me out of my predicament. I rushed to the Chamber of Commerce and the industry of Evry in France. Two weeks later, my company was created. A new

French law had just been issued on financial support for young graduates from graduate schools who wished to engage in business. I was the perfect fit for the selection, and I believed I had a chance to make it!

I met several funding agencies accredited by the government for young graduates of my group. I filled out files after files, I provided documents after documents. Unfortunately, I was never able to obtain the money I needed, nor the financial support the French Government promised to start my project and I found myself at square one.

What was I going to do? Little by little I became cognizant of the growing discrimination against the professional development of immigrants in French institutions and companies. From that time, something began to boil in me. Subsequently I created an association in France, whose goal was to recognize the skills and talents of black women, to enhance their work and lead them to take their destiny into their own hands.

I needed to do something for black women facing the same frustrations and problems I had. I had to sound the alarm.

We can count thousands of women who, like me, have ideas, do ingenious things, and remain unknown, in the shadows. Through their hard work, they are the driving force of their country's economy.

African women are the backbone of the rural economy in much of sub-Saharan Africa. About 80% of the economically active female workforce is employed in agriculture, and women constitute about 47% of the total agricultural workforce. Currently, the resources and dynamism provided by women and girls are not considered in the calculation of the gross domestic product. This underestimation of the African national economic resources has a negative influence on investment and modernization priorities. Sectors in which women work informally (food industry, domestic hydraulic, pharmaceutical industry, hardware...) are not listed on the priorities of national investments index.

Within the framework of the organization I created, I introduced in 2004 in Cameroon, the first ceremony of the Palms for the Excellence of Women. A ceremony designed to promote the talents of women in all sectors of activities. I understood the African woman has an important contribution to make to the world. She needed especially to be aware of what she represents on the continental and global chessboard. By the position she occupies in the African economy, the woman must take her role seriously and become more involved in the boards of major local companies and Government institutions.
In America, the issue of the positioning of black women in society is also serious. They are stereotyped by the media and society, they are perceived as "being overweight, loud, and lazy, live on social assistance, have many children by different fathers, and uneducated". Yet, despite the

discrimination, the African American women are establishing themselves on the business stage and have more and more success. Though they are not honored in the media, they are showing the world alike the other races of women they are smart and have much to give to the world.

My encounter with Sandra Monthieux Pelage

Following this event pioneered in Cameroon on December 2004, I contacted Sandra Monthieux Pelage, this charming lady from Martinique who is at the origin of the English translation of *Hommage à la Femme Noire*, (*In praise of Black woman*) book in 6 volumes, from the author Simone Schwarz-Bart of Guadeloupean origin. Sandra Monthieux Pelage made the recognition of women's talents and the contribution of black woman to the world her *leitmotiv*. Serving this cause for more than seven years gave birth to the World Congress of Black Women Leader in Paris in 2004, congress to which I also participated.

We got our act together and agreed on the status of the black woman who was ultimately very isolated, and who did not have a very high profile. We both believed the African woman whether from the Diaspora or the continent was not always aware of the importance of the contribution she could have worldwide. Sandra and I quickly agreed to work together and to organize the second edition of the

Congress of Black Women Leader she was planning to launch in Houston, Texas in October 2005 in the United States.

Working alongside Sandra was a learning experience. I learned how to work with someone who has a personality, an intellectual stature and relevant geo-strategic knowledge.

I was passionate about her views which were about promoting the black woman leader in the world; as a young ambitious black woman, I was motivated. Only, I had the burden for this African woman, this black woman who is not a leader, who has something to give, to assert and to learn. This black woman who is playing a role in the national, regional and even global economic chessboard, but who is ignored. This woman was also part of this global movement.

After the Congress of Houston, the results were not great. From 800 people who participated in Paris in 2004, we only reached approximately 50 people maximum in Houston. This was a failure! The reasons for this failure still escape me to this day; however, participants kept a good memory of the event. I saw Sandra in Paris again a few months after this experience, then I lost touch with her; for me, she was still in Houston in the US.

Patricia Esther Secke

Sandra has a responsibility in this fight, in this mission on the grounds that God has endowed her with complementary talents. I pray that the promise of God brings her back, and his work be done. Back in Paris, several participants from Africa and Europe suggested I continue this initiative with the objective of creating a network of black women from all social strata, to initiate real society projects.

In 2006, I was far from imagining that raising awareness, promoting and bringing black women from around the world together for the building of Africa and its integrated diaspora, would be my mission. I received in a dream specific instruction on the continuation of this unfinished work. I heard a voice tell me: "I want you to do the following: organize Congresses of black women, and continue with this unfinished work" a little worried I simply answered: "But Lord, I am not conversant with this work and where will I start? In addition, Sandra will tell everyone I have taken her concept". The reassuring voice told me: "don't worry about Sandrah, she will work alongside you."

Thus, I launched myself in the organization of the First International Congress of Black Women, held in January 2007 in Paris at the complex of the Grande arche de la défense. A new name which incorporated women non-leaders, destined to each become competitive in her area of activities. It was about integrating black women of all social strata and the whole world.

Today we move towards the achievement of these objectives, and I pray with all my heart for Sandra Monthieux Pelage and her family. I pray for her children and for the hand of God to rest on their lives. They were residing in Houston, Texas in the US, place where they lived for many years. But today, no one knows exactly where she is with her family. May God protect them!

My divorce

In 2005, I had to get a divorce from my husband. We had many misunderstandings in our couple in that my husband didn't encourage me in my mission and didn't perceive me as a visionary. He was especially unwilling to have me launch into this project. We had to separate on friendly terms. It was the only solution, since it was impossible for me to stop my vision, and it was impossible for him to live with a woman who claimed to have large projects for Africa.

Patricia Esther Secke

Chapter 2: My CONVERSION

The circumstances which led me to Jesus: The First International Congress of Black Women in 2007.

Chapter 2: My CONVERSION

The circumstances which led me to Jesus: The First International Congress of Black Women in 2007.

Enthusiastic and very thrilled at the idea of organizing the International Congress of Black Women, I surrounded myself with a team which seemed suitable: this team consisted of people I knew as professionals, voluntary friends, yet without much experience. Being a novice in the business world and naive, I trusted everyone, and the recommendations made to me for the success of the Congress too fast.

Result: for a first endeavor, the Congress was a success in terms of the attendance. We had three hundred women from diverse backgrounds participating in the event. We had keynote speakers with compelling themes, some female ministers and two first ladies of Africa.

However, financially it was a disaster, the balance was "one hundred and sixty-five thousand Euros of debts" a deficit of 165.000 Euros.

The day following the Congress, I soon realized I was in serious trouble, facing this financial disaster alone. The friends I had and could rely on all disappeared. Anxiety was growing while the creditors were harassing me by certified mail and over the phone. I was receiving on-going threats and indescribable pressure. I was wondering how I reached this point.

One day I was behind the wheel of my car, driving without knowing where I was going, until I reached a roundabout. I drove in circles several times and I exclaimed myself: Lord show me the way; I don't know where to go. What am I going to do? How do I rectify this situation? Or where will I find 165 000 euros to pay off my debts not including my daily survival needs? I was not out of the woods yet! What did I commit myself to? How did I get to this point?

Without being aware of it, I had prayed the prayer God asks us to pray when we are in distress: "Call unto me, and I will answer thee, and show thee great and mighty things, which thou knowest not". Jeremiah 33, verse 3, God heard my cry and a friend, Sandra Lecefel called me to tell me she had seen me in a dream the night before, I was in a coffin, but not dead. She told me I needed prayers and invited me to attend a prayer meeting one Wednesday in the month of February 2007.

I went, there were about 10 people, they prayed for me and I went back home. A few days later, my friend Isabelle Kiti invited me to her church in the Paris area in the suburb of Montrouge, and this is where I received Jesus Christ as my Lord and Savior. It was the beginning of my walk in the knowledge of the word of God: The Bible.

Jesus Christ is the way, the truth, and the life. It is only in Him one can fulfill one's destiny on this earth. There are blessings we receive only when we are in Jesus. If you are reading this book and you have not yet received Jesus Christ as Lord and Savior, I invite you to do so and you'll see the glory of God in your life. You will fulfill your dreams, even those which appear impossible, because with God everything is possible.

Six months after accepting to walk with Jesus Christ as my Savior, I was growing up gently in my faith through teachings, exhortations and the reading of the bible.

I used to drink brandy and I took red wine with every meal. When people made comments about my taste for alcohol, I used the excuse that Jesus turned water into wine, and it was a good reason to keep on drinking.

Until the day when, in my sleep, a voice woke me up around 5am and very clearly, I heard this voice quote accurately the following verse: "Isaiah 5 verse 22". Surprise, I said internally "but what is this?" I decided to go back to sleep telling myself "I would look for this passage when my alarm clock will ring". But I couldn't go back to sleep, I turned on the light, I opened my bible and discovered with amazement this verse I will never forget: "Woe unto them that are mighty to drink wine, and men of strength to mingle strong drink". Isaiah 5 verse 22.

I was amazed! I wondered how it was possible for God to know us in such a fundamental way, in our deepest flaws. Indeed, I had valor and bravery to drink red wine and I was drinking cognac which is very strong liquor. God himself came to speak to me personally, without intermediaries. "I understood I was binging, and I should take this warning seriously."

I had already received the mission God had assigned me, but I thought I could go on living like before. Live like someone who had not been set apart, living by the laws and habits of this world, fulfilling my desires as I wanted to. Nevertheless, I understood later that once you receive a call from on high, (of God) it is a Holy calling. It is something sacred which must be jealously protected from any compromise or smear. I discerned that being elected by God was not an end itself, but a journey which required time devoted to a spiritual stripping and a life of sanctification.

Our God calls its elected representatives to sanctification in Leviticus 10 verses 9 and 10, it is written: "Do not drink wine nor strong drink, thou, nor thy sons with thee, when ye go into the tabernacle of the congregation, lest ye die: it shall be a statute forever throughout your generations: and that ye may put difference between holy and unholy, and between unclean and clean, which is unclean that which is pure".

We are for God, a royal priesthood, a people set apart for his purposes. The chosen people of God must not live anyhow. We have been created in the image and likeness of God. We are so valuable in his eyes that he told us in Proverbs chapter 31 verse 4: "it is not for Kings to drink wine, nor to the princes to seek strong liquors".

I have always wondered why God had allowed some people to drink wine by offering the water turned into wine, but I understood later why: God has his elected ones with whom he works, and those must achieve a certain level of sanctification enabling them to accomplish things for God on Earth. Proverbs 31 verse 14: "by me Kings Reign, and princes ordered what is right". God calls his elected to reign with him on this earth, and to order his justice, that is why he says: "I confirm the word of my servant, and I made that predict my envoys" Isaiah 44, verse 26.

After reading this warning on alcohol in Isaiah 5 verse 22, I was puzzled for several days. However, I kept drinking cognac and wine. One night, I poured myself half of a small glass of cognac with the warning more vivid in my mind. This passage from the bible rang in my mind like a bell in such a way that I ended up looking extensively at the bottle which was two meters away from me and said: "cognac, I separate myself from you, because I choose to obey the voice I've heard" I took the bottle of cognac and emptied it in the kitchen sink. And I've never drank cognac to this day. It happened in July 2007.

Patricia Esther Secke

After this rupture from cognac, I persisted however in drinking red wine with my meals thinking it wasn't doing any harm since it is not as strong as liquor. As an excuse I used the passage of scripture where the Apostle Paul recommended a little wine to Timothy: "Drink no longer water but use a little wine for thy stomach's sake and thine often infirmities". 1Timothy 5, verse 23.

I convinced myself I had a good reason to drink wine when referring to this verse. Yet when I read it carefully in view of my situation, I had to acknowledge I didn't have any stomach problems and I had no common ailment.

Up to February 12, 2008 which was the day I had another visitation of the God of covenant. God, who had set me apart, came a second time to speak to me and said: "my daughter, don't you know you are my miracle? And I will make you a miracle?" I felt like a heat had invaded me, and I started crying about my sins, I replied: "Yes father, I know it....and then I heard: So, are you ready to stop drinking your glass of wine for me? Are you ready to be pure for me?" ...And I replied: "Yes Lord I'm ready".

God knows us. He knew I didn't stop drinking wine with my meals, though I already made the effort to stop drinking cognac. God is the God of "to will and to do so." This voice was so soft, full of affection, love and compassion, it was impossible to resist Him.

God is merciful, he is love, and when he makes a covenant, he brings a promise to fulfill his part of the contract. God wanted to use me as an instrument through which he would accomplish his purposes. His promise was he would do miracles through me, and his condition, which is my part of the contract, is that I be pure for him. Pure to receive Him, pure to discern what he expects from me, pure to be equipped for my mission, and pure to receive the tools necessary to operate in the corridor in which he predestined me.

Our covenant was reached! I don't drink a drop of alcohol anymore. I know one thing, which is that I will never fail no matter the pitfalls of the enemy. Even if I walk in the Valley of the shadow of death, I will fear no evil because his rod, his staff and his promise comfort me. Praise the Lord, forever and ever, Amen!

Chapter 3

THE BEGINNING OF MY CONSECRATION

Chapter 3: THE BEGINNING OF MY CONSECRATION

The first thing Jesus did in me when I got converted was that he filled my heart with peace. He is the prince of peace and gives peace which passes all understanding. Despite all the problems surrounding me, I had the hope everything would eventually get resolved. I knew Jesus would take care of all my burdens, as he promised by saying: "Come unto me, all ye that labour and are heavy laden and I will give you rest. Take my yoke upon you and learn of me; for I am meek and lowly in heart: and ye shall find rest unto your souls. For my yoke is easy, and my burden is light". Matthew 11: 28-30.

I had peace and I was prepared to receive the instructions of Jesus. I had an inexplicable thirst to know him. I wanted to listen to him, receive him and know this Jesus who had given me such wholesome peace. I was no longer sleeping as much, Tuesday and Friday I was attending the Bible study, on Sunday I was at Church. I spent sleepless nights listening to teachings on websites such as www.enseignemoi.com and www.topchretien.com. I would spend whole days at home without stepping out. I needed God. I was reading teachings on the internet, on faith, on the walk with God to consecration, sanctification, the glory of God, and God's will.

Patricia Esther Secke

My financial woes were not resolved, I still had debts. I had no stable job, but I had peace, inexplicable peace, a peace which friends, family, and the world does not give, but that only Jesus Christ gives.

Little by little, I began to be released from the grip of worldly things, and from the attitudes the Holy Scriptures prohibit but accommodated everyone. I got rid of all the entertainment and parties' friends I had, and which finally could not replace the treasure I came to discover and receive in Jesus Christ.

I also disconnected myself from my circle of friends. Finally, we no longer shared the same interests, the same conversations and the same way of seeing things. I was more and more uncomfortable in nightclubs, and I stopped going there. I drifted in my quest for the Lord. I was more and more solitary, and I avoided unhealthy conversations: gossips, critics, lies, disputes, manipulations.

When there is no fear of God, people tend to lie easily and free of charge, sometimes, those lies are not necessary. Jesus Christ is the truth. He is defined as the truth. Those who claim to be Christians and claim to walk with Jesus should not lie. If this happens, they should repent immediately.

Due to this desire for consecration to God, I found myself in a church where the biblical teachings were deeper. I needed to expand my knowledge in the Holy Scriptures and know the mind of God. We must be sensitive to the leading of the Holy Spirit. Before changing church, I was in a church where they greatly criticized the pastoral couple, especially the wife of the pastor. I was part of the people who criticized along with my favorite sisters in Christ. There were clicks and groups in the church. But I soon began to feel discomfort and unease in this atmosphere. On the days where the pastor called for peace in the church preaching a message of repentance to give up the clicks, there was peace in the church, yet the same evening people were back to gossiping again.

I remember taking the decision to leave this church without being influenced by anyone. Indeed, I had not told my friends I was planning to leave. I felt deep within me that in order to grow in my faith, I needed to go into the depths of God for the mission which awaited me.

My place was elsewhere.

After Sunday's service, I left the church knowing I would never be back, although I did not know where to go the following Sunday. On Saturday evening while going to bed, I asked the Lord to lead me and tell me where he wanted me to worship the next day. When I woke up on Sunday morning, I didn't hear any bell sound. Then, I said in a loud voice, Lord, where do I meet you this morning? I heard this sweet voice tell me "there is a church few meters from here, go there".

By faith, I went there. In this church which is called "Eglise de la Louange", God had everything prepared, biblical teachings were given in small groups, two or three times per week and by level. Church leaders were available. The Holy Spirit truly began to transform me through teachings, the power of the word, so my faith started to grow. The children of God perish due to a lack of teaching and knowledge of the word of God. To be free from the yoke of this hostile world in which we live and the upcoming tribulations, we must take the word of God seriously and apply it. It is the ignorance of the purpose of the word of God that leads us to sin, to rebellion against God's precepts and to defying his commands.

Ignorance kills human, Hosea chapter 4 and verse 6 says: "My people are destroyed for lack of knowledge: because thou hast rejected knowledge, I will also reject thee, that thou shalt be no priest to me: seeing thou hast forgotten the law of thy God, I will also forget thy children". The lack of knowledge of God and his will kill man. The will of God is in his word which is the bible.

All the situations we face in the world are clearly presented in the bible, and all the solutions are also found there. Human sciences and degrees show that man is gifted and zelous in his secular knowledge of the world, without so far trying to know the word of God which the source of all things is. The Holy Scriptures taught me that a medical doctor has the knowledge, but by practicing abortion, he commits a murder, and it could be a stumbling block for his patient which may later pay the consequences by sterility. A lawyer knows the law, but by pleading the cause of a guilty party practices lies. The lack of science is not good for man, but science must not be the mistress of man. Proverbs 19 verses 2 to 3: "Also, that the soul be without knowledge, it is not good; and he that hasteth with his feet sinneth. The foolishness of man perverteth his way: and his heart fretteth against the LORD".

The ignorance of the laws of God leads to rebellion and the consequences of sin cause a rift in the communion between God and man. Man is separated from God. There isn't any contact with God, any face to face. God hides his face to man and his prayer becomes an abomination. Spiritual death ensues, translated by atheism, disbelief, the doubt of the God's existence, idolatry, and religions. This spiritual death caused by sin can become eternal if the sinner does not repent and is not willing to change his behavior.

Patricia Esther Secke

Sin is the root cause of human woes. The sinful man by losing the status of child of God is bound and became Satan's slave: "Jesus answered them, verily, verily, I say unto you; whosoever committed sin is the servant of sin". John 8 verse 34.

I was also taught, by the grace of God, about the practices which bound men. I received some teaching about the different forms of sins and their consequences in our lives: debauchery and its derivatives (theft, embezzlement, fraud, lies, gluttony, smoking, drunkenness, greed, avarice) about idolatry (worship or serve the creature instead of the creator) idolatrous practices and forms such as: participating in worldly associations, having familiar objects of idolatry in the house, consuming Earth clay, possessing books on magic and occult sciences, some gifts received from certain people, objects won from games of chance, objects with the Zodiac insignia, Eastern religions objects, the cure of water, Indian mushrooms, images and articles representing celestial beings, the cross of Jesus, the holy water, some family objects promising wealth.

All those practices may be the consequences of the turmoil and bondages in our lives, and God has been clear and firm on those practices: "Thou shalt have no other gods before me. Thou shalt not make unto thee any graven image, or any likeness of anything that is in heaven above, or that is in the earth beneath, or that is in the water under the earth. Thou shalt not bow down thyself to them, nor serve them: for I the LORD thy God am a jealous God, visiting the iniquity of the fathers upon the children unto the third and fourth generation of them that hate me; and shewing mercy unto thousands of them that love me, and keep my commandments." Exodus 20, verse 3 to 6.

Let's keep the commandments of the Lord to ensure blessings for our children, and for our posterity up to a thousand generations.

I remember at the time I diligently attended the traditional church, I bought many books on prayers regarding the prayers to the saints, prayers to saint Charlemagne, saint Rita for hopeless causes, saint Theresa of the child Jesus, St. Anthony for people wanting children, books on white magic, on the novenas of prayer which required lighting some candles, or praying with a rosary, etc.

These forms of prayers in light of the word of God are considered as magical arts. Since the bible tells us there is only one who is holy: Jesus Christ, who said "I am the way, the truth and the life; no one comes to the father except through me". This means the only intermediary and mediator between God and man is Jesus, since he died on the cross of Calvary to reconcile men with God, and made us free from the yoke of Satan, by paying the price for the reconciliation through his blood.

The rift between God and I caused me to look for him outside of his word, in the books of the saints, and by doing endless novenas. I was looking for the power in these prayers rituals by lighting candles and using the rosary. It is written in the bible to grow in power, we must abandon, renounce these practices and put the word of God in practice: Acts 19, verse 18 and 19: "And many that believed came, and confessed, and shewed their deeds. Many of them also which used curious arts brought their books together and burned them before all men: and they counted the price of them and found it fifty thousand pieces of silver".

At the beginning of my conversion, it was difficult for me to forgive some things, some injustice committed against me. However, the teachings I received on forgiveness made me realize it is important to forgive those who offend us so that God may also forgive us the offenses we commit against others. Forgiveness strengthens the effectiveness of our prayers and fills us with the same compassion Jesus had when he said in Luke 23, verse 34: "Father forgive them for they do not know what they do". Forgiveness is a powerful source of release. Forgiveness releases the move of the Holy Spirit. God moves mightily through a prayer made in a spirit of truth. Forgiveness is the fundamental condition for a genuine communion between God and man. If you have forgiven, your prayer will be answered.

The studies and teachings learned on deliverance did me much good and opened my eyes in my ongoing walk with the Lord. Only God delivers! Deliverance is the total freedom of a person who lived under satanic or demonic slavery: "Stand fast therefore in the liberty wherewith Christ hath made us free and be not entangled again with the yoke of bondage". Galatians 5, verse 1.

If today, the people of God remain miserable, it is because they are neither free nor delivered. Jesus set us free that we might be free indeed. It is therefore essential to know the key to freedom, which is the word of God as it is indicated in John 8, verse 32: "you will know the truth and the truth shall set you free". Deliverance is essential for any human being, for every Christian today. The devil is present even in the Christian congregations. Many children of God live in chains from satanic bondages. They are chained like goats by long strings, though they can travel a good distance as if they were free, yet in reality they are under the influence of the power of darkness. They do not live in peace. Their lives are not changing, and the oppression of the world burdens them. Deliverance comes from God; it is divine and not human.

Patricia Esther Secke

I lived previously in an environment where the laws of God were not respected. I needed deliverance for my mentality to be renewed. I cried out to God, and I had laid my problems at his feet sincerely. I confessed everything to him directly and without hiding my sins, I was repenting, humbling myself before God as the Holy Scriptures suggest: "...know thou the God of thy father, and serve him with a perfect heart and with a willing mind: for the LORD searcheth all hearts, and understandeth all the imaginations of the thoughts: if thou seek him, he will be found of thee; but if thou forsake him, he will cast thee off forever." 1 Chronicles 28, verse 9.

Being increasingly strengthened in my faith and starting to take the word of God seriously, I felt deep within myself the need to be baptized. Through the teachings, I understood the importance of water baptism and the baptism of the Holy Spirit. It is through water baptism we become part of the Church, the body of Christ, since it is Jesus who is the head of the church. The church is not a building. The church is all true Christians. It is through water baptism we can access the promised blessings of the Lord: "those who believe and who will be baptized will be saved, but those who do not believe will be condemned". Mark 16, verse 16

Any commitment goes first through repentance, by renouncing what was previously: renounce sin and the rest will be done by the grace of God. It is God who confirms this commitment by the baptism of the Holy Spirit as indicated in the book of the Acts of the Apostles. Acts 2, verse 38: "Repent, and be baptized every one of you in the name of Jesus Christ for the remission of sins, and ye shall receive the gift of the Holy Ghost".

In committing to serve God, I agreed to pay the price. I don't do what I want to do, but I do what the one who committed himself to me wants me to do. I pledged to forsake what I was doing to embrace the vision God showed me and asked me to fulfill. As everywhere else, a commitment is followed by a gesture or a contract as well as visible (men) and invisible (Angels and demons) witnesses.

During my water baptism, I pledged to put the word of God into practice by the grace of God and the strength of the Holy Spirit (since I am not able to do it on my own), it is for this reason I received the Holy Spirit to enable me to walk in sanctification, and God committed himself to watch over me. My commitment is called water baptism. I personally take the commitment to follow the ways of Jesus.

When God commits to me, he replies by the baptism of the Holy Spirit manifested by the fruit of the Spirit, which is permanent joy and the gift of the spirit, which is the speaking in tongues. The gifts of the spirit lead to the fear of God and the spirit of God personally edifies me. The symbol of immersion represents the death of the members that cause us to sin. Spiritually, our body is dead to sin. It will no longer be comfortable in sin. It is mainly repentance which will lead us, and the baptism will help us walk in sanctification and flee sin.

We become one same plant with Jesus. Exiting the water, sin remains in the water and we come out with a newness of life. When God looks at us, he sees Christ. We are called to be the extension of the glory of God on this earth. We must not play with our salvation. God is an unlimited God who can give us everything we want. My daily prayer is for God to keep me pure, loyal to him in a hostile world. We live in challenging times, where confusion reigns, and where the truth seems to have been veiled.

Without the will and the power of God, we cannot do anything. He is the one who inclines our hearts for the Holy Spirit to teach us all truth.

All these lessons have built me up and helped me in the process of my consecration to God. By forsaking the pleasures of the world, and selfish desires, I had the strength to persevere. God is faithful and still behind his word to perform it. He is not going to tempt us beyond our strength because he is love and he knows when we are willing to follow him. My consecration to God and to the mission he has entrusted me continue on a daily basis. I need to be more devoted through prayer, to follow his instructions, his directions, recommendations, and to hear his voice. Since Jesus said: "my sheep hear my voice; I know them, and they follow me" John 10 verse 27.

The beginning of my consecration occurred during serious hardship from February 2007 to September 2008. A year and a half of adverse circumstances enabled me to learn from God. God had created a vacuum around me to train me and prepare me for the mission he had for me. God brought me to a total state of dependency on him. I needed to give him my all, in order to receive his fullness. God made me sever all my ties with the world for me to possess everything in his Kingdom.

God sets us apart to equip us for war, because Jesus said: "Think not that I am come to send peace on earth: I came not to send peace, but a sword". Matthew 10:34.
We live in a world led by the devil that is determined to destroy us, degrade us and make us lose our dignity as children of God created in the image of God. We live in a time of tribulations and conspiracy where the Lord needs the real faithful ones for his work. We live in evil days. World news shows us facts relating to the signs of the end of time: the crisis in Africa, the Middle East, terrestrial natural disasters taking place today and which will still tumble in the

world in the days to come. The wars, the noises of war, torment, false prophets, a nation standing up against a nation and a kingdom rising up against a kingdom are all additional signs of the end of time.

God needs true disciples, an army set apart to be equipped with all the weapons necessary to overcome on this earth. And to do so, we must walk in the truth, carry the torch of justice, and walk in the word of God and according to the following strategic statement of war: Ephesians 6, verse 10 to 18: "Finally, my brethren, be strong in the Lord, and in the power of his might. Put on the whole armor of God that ye may be able to stand against the wiles of the devil. For we wrestle not against flesh and blood, but against principalities, against powers, against the rulers of the darkness of this world, against spiritual wickedness in high places. Wherefore take unto you the whole armor of God that ye may be able to withstand in the evil day, and having done all, to stand. Stand therefore, having your loins girt about with truth, and having on the breastplate of righteousness; And your feet shod with the preparation of the gospel of peace; Above all, taking the shield of faith, wherewith ye shall be able to quench all the fiery darts of the wicked. And take the helmet of salvation, and the sword of the Spirit, which is the word of God: Praying always with all prayer and supplication in the Spirit, and watching thereunto with all perseverance and supplication for all saints;"

If we do not walk according to this strategic instruction of war given by the word of God, we will have a hard time extinguishing fiery darts of the wicked one, on this earth and in this "jungle" which is the apostasy of the end of time. Despite multiple prayers and the number of years spent every Sunday at church, without sanctification we will lose the war and then the world will ask, where is your God?

The practical implementation of the commandments of God has helped me to quickly come out of the difficulties and the impasse in which I was. I gradually discovered the beauty of God, his size, his power and I received extraordinary revelations.

Patricia Esther Secke

Chapter 4

GOD IS A GOD OF COVENANT AND MIRACLES

Chapter 4: GOD IS A GOD OF COVENANT AND MIRACLES

WILDERNESS AND TOTAL IMPASSE

I had received Jesus Christ as my Lord and my Savior, and I was determined to walk in consecration. However, I still had 165 000 Euros of debts following the first Congress of black women I organized in 2007: part of the registration fees of the participants was embezzled by the event agency in charge of the organization of the Congress. I trusted them just to realize later they charged me 40 000 Euros for the Conference Hall of the "Grande Arche de la defense" in Paris, when the rental space costs only 11 000 Euros. Caterers overbilled the meals to 20 000 Euros per meal for 2 days. Several women had participated without paying for the registration fees or the meals.

A delegation of 25 women from Africa and supported financially by the President of their country didn't pay off their bill of about 15 000 Euros, which included unpaid hotel fees, meals consumed, training for which our organization made reservations for. One African lady from Gabon offered to contribute to the success of the Congress by the looking for sponsors.

Two cosmetics companies agreed to contribute up to 5000 Euros each and we were to give her a commission of 1500 Euros per contract signed. She collected ten thousand Euros directly from the corporations and disappeared. And this without counting the cost for the booths occupied by the participants who chose not to pay for their booth rental fees. It was a total confusion; I discovered the world in which I lived.

Alone in this impasse, I experienced rejection from my family, abandonment from few friends and all sorts of setbacks such as the suspension of my banking privileges. I no longer had a bank account, my car was without insurance for lack of means, and sometimes I only had two or five Euros in my pocket which was just enough to eat a box of white beans and rice.

Only God could bring me out of this chaotic situation. I prayed day and night. I meditated on the word of God; I went to church every day it was open. I spent hours in prayer, no one could help me. The friends, who called to inquire about me, were more interested in finding out whether I had been able to pull through. One Sunday while leaving the church after a joyful service, I was happy, filled with hope and very confident in God for the resolution of my problems soon. Walking to my car, I noticed my left rear-view mirror had been stolen, (the perfect recipe to steal my joy and make me bitter and discouraged), but the word I had heard was so engrained in me that I look at the base where the mirror had been stolen, and said: "Satan do not think you're going to rob me of my joy today. I am sure that God is with me".

Another evening, on my way home I realized my electric power had been disconnected while I had not received any bill; tired of this oppression, I broke down in tears, I cried to God, I cried, and while I was crying, the word of Jesus resonated in my ear in a reassuring manner: "you will have tribulations in this world, but take courage, I have overcome the world". As if energy had been injected in me, I came out of my lamentations, I jumped from my seat, jumped on the phone, and I called the electricity company EDF to know what was going on. Someone understanding on the phone told me he did not know the cause of this disconnection which was not justified. He sent a technician who restored the power half an hour later.

I used my car only to go to Church. A Tuesday night on my way back from a prayer meeting, and singing hymns, I came out on a roundabout with at least ten police cars with police officers checking all passing cars: I had no car insurance for 6 months (which is forbidden by the law in France and is liable for immobilization of the vehicle) and my left rear view mirror which had been stolen a few weeks ago was not replaced. I exclaimed myself once it was my turn to be checked: "Lord Jesus, only you can get out me of this trap".

Once I reached the level of the female police officer who was checking me, I barely opened the window of the car when she told me: "go ahead mam! Escape!" I went hurtling off without being told twice and I went praising and thanking Jesus who had brought me out of a situation which would have resulted in the mobilization of my car, along with a heavy fine. My faith had saved me, as Jesus said himself in these cases: "Go thy way thy faith has saved you" Luke 7 verse 50.

One Sunday, I had to go to church, though I didn't have a penny to put gas in my car. I asked the Lord till when am I going to stay in this wilderness? The soft voice of the Holy Spirit told me "you have ten Euros in your bags, search your house," I casually went there since I had already looked into all my bags since the beginning of my hardships, and I knew I had nothing. I am looking in one, two, three, four, five bags, I find nothing, and I said, "but there is nothing in these bags", I mean "look in the grey bag, open the closure". I opened the closure of the grey bag and what do I see? Ten Euros. Alleluia! These ten Euros were like a fortune to me, I was happy to be able to go and listen to the word of God once again.

I want to thank my friends Isabelle and Timothy Kiti who have supported me greatly during these difficult times. Many times, they filled up the tank of my car, and several times they provided enough for me to be fed for weeks. May God richly bless this couple and remember them in his mercy and according to his promise: "Verily I say unto you, this generation shall not pass, till all these things be fulfilled. Heaven and earth shall pass away, but my words shall not pass away. But of that day and hour knoweth no man, no, not the angels of heaven, but my Father only". Matthew 25: 34-36

I also would like to thank one of my older sister and friend Mrs. Mame Coumba MBAYE in France. This woman with a big heart was by my side during the same period and supported me tremendously. I pray that God supports her in her life and in all her projects. God is true and He does not fail.

Patricia Esther Secke

Chapter 5

THE POWER OF GOD

Chapter 5: THE POWER OF GOD

GOD CANCELS MY DEBT OF 165,000 EUROS IN COURT

I found myself in Court for my debts which amounted to 165 000 euros: it was about finding out whether the French law authorized me to resume leading my organization without paying this huge debt.

The plea of my lawyer was to demonstrate the relevance of the noble task I was endeavoring to accomplish for the African community, and to explain to the jury that I had been set up by the businesspeople and the dishonest people I took as partners.

In September 2007, on the day of the hearing, my lawyer asked me in the waiting room how I planned to direct my career professionally following the decision of the judge. I handed him a magazine in which I had given an interview the previous month; it was written "2th International Congress of the Black Woman 2008". Puzzled, he told me: "you are not going to continue, seeing the mess in which you are" I replied I was actually going to pursue my mission since I've stolen no one and I know God is the just judge, he will justify me. Then my lawyer asked me not to speak about the second Congress at the hearing for fear the judge may take some sanctions against me.

Patricia Esther Secke

After the hearing, the judge decided to give his final decision couple of months later. Normally I couldn't officially announce the second Congress without having the judge's final decision. Time went by, we were already in September 2007 and the second Congress was set for April 2008. I had seven months to set everything in motion.

I contacted a friend of my mother's, Anne, who leads a Parisian insurance firm and supported and greatly encouraged me in this mission. I spoke to her about my intent to announce the second Congress, she encouraged me! Only my organization "AQuarius International France" was in litigation, I couldn't do anything under that name, neither in my own name. Then I suggested to Anne to create another organization with her as the President, and me as General coordinator of the project, since I came up with the vision.

We reached an agreement. Through much reflection and pondering on the mission God had given me, and the new directions of the work, I prepared and introduced the files for the creation of the new organization, and "Africa Femmes Performantes was born". I was pleased to pursue my dream. However, I was facing blackmail again! Fifteen days later, Anne as the new President of the organization, summoned me to her office and talked to me in these terms: "if I am President of your organization, you should come and work in my office here. I give you a space in the back of the room, so I can see how you work. You must give me the organization's checkbook. I must control all the transactions in the account since you're a very bad manager and I do not want my name mixed up with your debt's records".

I was deeply hurt, I told her I was going to make the necessary arrangements, and I stepped out of her office. In my car I bursted into tears, I cried to God, and I told him: "Lord, hear how they deal with me your daughter, I cancel all these wrong words declared over me and I said I will not be subject to any control whatsoever, no blackmail, I will make it because the God I pray is not any kind of God".

That evening I went to church, the sermon preached was for me. He said: "God is waiting for you, at the place where you derailed from, while you were both walking together". Why trust men when your God is powerful? "Obey, submit yourself completely to God and you'll see, he will open doors that you can't even imagine".

I left the church full of strength, courage, faith and the Holy Ghost reminded me this word of Jesus Christ on my way back: "he who does not bear his cross and does not follow me is not worthy to be my disciple" Matthew 10 verse 38.

Patricia Esther Secke

My decision was taken: Court's ruling or not, Jesus Christ was asking me as a disciple, to follow the mandate he had given me sovereignly. Therefore, I should not move according to the laws and the ultimatums of men.

I undertook the administrative procedures. I established all the official documents of "Africa Femmes Performantes" in my name and as founding President. God has mandated me. There was no reason to rely on a third party which didn't understand anything about the mandate God had given me to represent me. I sent an email to Anne to let her know I released her from her fears and that I had taken the commitment to bear my cross and follow God.

Couple of days later, all the official documents were in my name. I was with Amina my collaborator. We supported each other in prayer and entrusted everything to God. Through a step of faith, I was able to address the concern about being controlled and oppressed by someone God had not placed on my side.

Chapter 6:

GOD CLEARS MY NAME FROM THE SUSPENSION OF BANKING PRIVILEGES RECORDS IN FRANCE

Chapter 6: GOD CLEARS MY NAME FROM THE SUSPENSION OF BANKING PRIVILEGES RECORDS IN FRANCE

After this first feat, a mountain stood before us: she and I had our banking privileges suspended. We had a record with the Bank of France and were prohibited from opening a bank account. Nevertheless, the organization absolutely needed an account to operate.

I took an appointment at the Bank, at the "Crédit Coopératif Bank" to open an account and I said to Amina: "I have carried my cross, I follow Jesus, he will do the rest" I asked her to pray with me and we prayed this prayer: "Lord, my sister Amina and I come in one accord before you, you said to Abraham to leave his homeland and go to a place you will show him and he obeyed you without knowing where he was going so you honored him...in the same way Lord, here we are with our banking privileges suspended, you asked me to carry my cross and follow you Lord and I have obeyed, now we are heading to the bank, open an account for us. Thank you, Lord, Amen".

Amina and I reached the Bank. The bank advisor welcomed us, and I immediately laid all my cards on the table saying: "Madam, I will be honest with you. My banking privileges have been suspended. We want to open the account of our organization and if it makes you uncomfortable to authorize me to have the bank signature authority in my capacity as President of the organization, I can mandate the treasurer to sign on behalf of the association".

This lady looked at me right in the eyes and replied: "But …I trust you…not only am I opening the account, but I give the bank account signature authority only to you!"

I had learned an important lesson. God has mandated me and no one else. Consequently, he gave me all the powers associated with this mandate. In my small human mind, suggesting to the advisor to bestow the bank account signature authority to someone else revealed my small-mindedness in thinking that God was not able to transcend the human laws and banking restrictions. I was still trying to find the solution, rather than letting God move. Additionally, God who searches the hearts knew the treasurer had accepted this position by convenience and not out of conviction seeing that a few months later she left the organization.

Alleluia! I was pleasantly surprised by this miracle. According to French law, to regularize the issue of the suspension of banking privileges, the incumbent must pay the amount owed to the bank to recover all his rights of use of a new account. I had not done so, yet all my banking rights were restored to me. Only God can move in this dimension. I was in joy and glad to have obeyed the Lord, he showed me His faithfulness. May He receive the glory! He is the master of time and circumstances.

Without further thought about the pending court's ruling that would decide the fate of the organization, we proceeded with the preparations for the second Congress.

The court's decision was issued on January 2008. The judge concluded that being a novice in the world of business and having confidence in all my collaborators and services providers for the organization of the Congress 2007, I had been swindled and duped. Therefore, the court gave me the authorization to pursue this noble and important cause for women and for society. Alleluia!

Gradually, I realized that obeying God against any obstacle was in fact building on the rock, Jesus Christ. I understood God who has called me to this faithful work, and this mission, will do it. I am merely an instrument he uses. I also had the confidence God would restore me and replace the years which had been stolen.

Chapter 7

GOD IS WATCHING OVER HIS WORD TO PERFORM IT

Chapter 7: GOD IS WATCHING OVER HIS WORD TO PERFORM IT

The second International Congress of Black Women was successfully held on April 2008 and it fostered many connections with women from diverse backgrounds.

Amelia is a woman God put on my side two months prior to the Congress. She was one of the speakers in the plenary session's panel. In our exchange and conversations, I told her the story of the head of the delegation of 25 women from Congo Brazzaville in the 2007 Congress who had her trip financed by the President of her country. Unfortunately, this lady who was leading the Congolese delegation did not honor her commitment to pay off the invoice of fifteen thousand Euros owed to our organization.

Amelia, who was working in Congo-Brazzaville, was committed to plead my case to the first lady of Congo. Unfortunately, this track didn't yield any result right away. She sent me an email to let me know she had tried everything without any success and wished me the best of luck in my future endeavors. The content of this mail brought two large tears on my cheeks. The hope of being reimbursed had led to an impasse. From my car I cried out to God: "Lord, you are the God who opened the Red Sea to set the children of Israel free from captivity, you are the God who sent them manna in the wilderness. The Lord who kept their shoes and clothing in a miraculous way, so that they didn't get worn out wandering for forty years in the wilderness... It is you I invoke Lord, the God who works miracles. I invoke you the true God. Answer me; restore me, because I am in this impasse".

A week later, I received a call from Amelia telling me: "Patricia, I have sixteen thousand Euros in my bag for you, given by the husband of the head of the delegation which had not paid the bill of fifteen thousand Euros from the 2007 congress". God is faithful! He said the thief will make a full restitution of what he stole. Exodus 22, verse 3.

I started paying off my debts and trusted God more and more. All the setbacks I went through as well as the miracles God performed to solve them, enabled me to be cognizant of the fact that God orchestrated my life. I am no longer surprised by circumstances and situations for his right hand is upon me, and he is God. I don't worry about the mist since I know behind the mist shines the morning star. I learned to remain silent and let God move.

Patricia Esther Secke

Chapter 8

THE BLESSINGS OF GOD ADD NO SORROW TO IT

Chapter 8: THE BLESSINGS OF GOD ADD NO SORROW TO IT

HOW GOD LED ME TO MY HUSBAND

Genesis 2, verse 22 And the rib, which the LORD God had taken from man, made he a woman, and brought her unto the man.

To better prepare for the third International Congress of Black Women scheduled in 2009 in Kinshasa in the Democratic Republic of the Congo, the idea came to me, with the invitation of Jeannine Scott, a remarkable powerful African-American woman who attended the 2008 Conference in Paris, to travel to the US in order to involve more African-American women in our projects.

I was preparing for this trip through many prayers. In July 2008, I went on a prayer retreat for a week in the Ardennes in Belgium because more and more I started to feel the burden of the task and the heavy responsibility of my mission which I had to bear alone. I felt lonely and needed to share this vision with a husband selected by God. In my prayers I said to God: "Lord, look, the mission you have entrusted to me is great and heavy, and I'm all alone striving to achieve it. Some felt I was too young for such a large mission; others thought I was quite inexperienced or not sufficiently equipped to carry out this vision. Others are still wondering why I have no husband.

Patricia Esther Secke

Give me Lord a husband who has an intellectual, physical and spiritual stature. He will be a great asset, helping me prepare my mission and bearing this vision with me".

In preparing the trip to Washington, DC I thought about going with a colleague to better organize this project. Curiously, the person who came to mind was Josette who lived in Congo-Brazzaville. She wondered why I picked her while I could have travelled with a collaborator from Paris who would not necessarily need to go through the hassle of obtaining a visa. I simply replied I felt deep within me that she was to accompany me. She obtained her visa and a week before our departure, she arrived in Paris. We spent some time in prayer together and on September 19, 2008, on our way to the airport, she said while taking her luggage: "I'm going to get you settled and I will come back". I watched her surprised by her comment and without making any remark, we left.

We arrived in Washington, DC on Saturday, September 20, 2008 and we were staying in Germantown in the state of Maryland near Washington, D.C. Our agenda and work program started on Monday, September 22. Therefore, we had the entire weekend to recuperate from the travel and jetlag. It was the opportunity for Josette to call one of her cousins she had not seen for more than twenty years. Our Sunday being free, her cousin came for a short visit and offered to give us a tour of the city, and then invited us for dinner at his house in Silver Spring.

One thing I learned with God is that nothing in our lives and walk with Jesus is done randomly. Very often, our actions, our reactions and our words are orchestrated by God. God has a wonderful plan for each of his children. When God wants to answer our prayers, no matter the way things occur, his will comes to pass. His ways are not our ways and God uses what he wants, when he wants, at the time he wants and where he wants to accomplish his purposes. God is sovereign! Did he not say in Isaiah 46, verse 11"Yea, I have spoken it, I will also bring it to pass; I have purposed it, I will also do it."

He also said: "my thoughts are not your thoughts and my ways are not your ways" Isaiah 55, verse 8.

Josette's cousin was named Leo, but for the respect I had for Josette who is a mature lady in her sixties, I called him "Uncle Leo".

After a delicious and hearty meal, "Uncle Leo" offered to give us a tour of his apartment which we admired greatly since it held a lot of charm and the décor was Louis XIV inspired. Once the tour was over, without knowing why, I expressed myself verbally as if marking my territory by saying: "listen Uncle Leo, we will move here because we feel good here. I won't return to Germantown; I will stay here". He simply and naturally responded "ok". Half an hour later, we were on our way to Germantown to retrieve our luggage and to settle down at "Uncle Leo's".

For three weeks, "Uncle Leo" showed a remarkable hospitality. I noticed he was very reserved, spoke very little, and smiled a lot. He was discreet and unobtrusive in his own house. I had been invited in a church where I prayed and listened to the word of God, I prayed much for "Uncle Leo" thanking the Lord for willing his heart to welcome us. I prayed for his life, and I asked God to reward him a hundredfold for his hospitality towards us every day.

The first Sunday I went to the Church; Josette came along with me. At the end of the service, we were warmly welcomed in the visitor's welcome center when Josette asked the pastor who ministered that day to pray for her. The Pastor actually prayed for her and couple of minutes later she found herself laying on the carpet. It seemed normal since many people receiving prayers in churches find themselves lying on the ground.

After this, ten minutes went by when Josette asked sister Audrey, who was praying for the sick of the church to pray for her. They were standing two meters away when Sister Audrey, as thrust by a force, got up and began to invoke the God who is Holy.

Then seized immediately by the spirit of revelation Audrey said in a loud voice while praying for Josette: "spirit of misery, begging, witchcraft, and spirit of divination, I cast you out in the name of Jesus Christ".

Chapter 9

WHEN THE WAYS OF A MAN SHALL PLEASE THE LORD, HE WILL CONVERT EVEN HIS ENEMIES TO PEACE.

Chapter 9: WHEN THE WAYS OF A MAN SHALL PLEASE THE LORD, HE WILL CONVERT EVEN HIS ENEMIES TO PEACE.

Spirit of witchcraft? Spirit of divination? I did not know my associate was oppressed by a spirit of divination; and this happened only a week after our arrival in Washington. I had to be cautious with the person I considered my best associate and the person who led me to the man God had chosen for me. The ways of God are not our ways!

The lesson I learned is that God is sovereign. He does what he wants, when he wants and with whom he wants for his own purposes. God can use our worst enemies to bless us, which is why we are recommended to love one another, and to forgive those who offend us seeing that our blessings could be in the hands of people we consider as enemies. Our blessings may therefore remain blocked as long as we view them as our enemies.

Similarly, when God places a witch on our side, and allows us to be made aware of that it is for us to show charity (fraternal love in Christ), to pray for him, to cast out the unclean spirit in him, and to preach the Gospel of Jesus Christ to him.

Audrey then dropped us home. Once we reached the entrance, Josette told Audrey "my husband was involved in the occult and Satanism, if I have slipped back into it, you must tell me!" Audrey replied that Pastor Moussa Touré was in charge of the deliverance ministry at church, and if she wished she could take her there. But Josette never went back for her deliverance.

We pursued our work program. We participated for several days in the Congress of Black Americans (Congressional Black Caucus). We participated in a forum of Exchange with the organization Africare, and many other professional meetings. I noticed something during our meetings, which was that Josette tried to advance her personal agenda, and that very often, she wanted me to do or say what she thought and wanted done. She was unaware of the fact that I walk with the vision I have received from God, and not according what people tell me to do. This was the first disagreement between us. After fifteen days, I was still compelled to be a little careful in view of what transpired regarding the state of her soul that day at church. I prayed a lot for her to be delivered from all bondages.

When leaving Paris, I had taken with me one of my notebooks where I recorded all my biblical teachings. I have a dozen of books, yet I don't know why I had taken a single book containing a teaching of Pastor Dorothy Rajah on the spirit of Jezebel. (May God keep using her to build-up the body of Christ!)

One evening, while re-reading my notes in this book, I reread this teaching about the spirit of Jezebel. I read again the definition of the spirit of Jezebel, and there, I understood my associate was a real Jezebel on my side.

The spirit of Jezebel is a spirit known in the bible, in the world. It is the spirit of the end of time. It is a spirit loosed and released on Earth. We need to be anointed by God to face it. This spirit is strong and seduces, it uses a lot of trickeries. The spirit of Jezebel operates among those who already have knowledge of it. It is a spirit which is in the church, which is very strong and powerful.

We live in the end time, one must be extremely cautious and discerning, considering the spirit of Jezebel is an idolatrous and a religious spirit, a political spirit, a spirit of manipulation, and concealment leading people into spiritual, moral and sexual perversion. This spirit aims to give to true pure Christians in their faith another spirit which is no longer the spirit of the Gospel. Everything referring to God is not necessarily of God.

It is a spirit which knows how to play with appearances, which works extensively on its image, appearance, in its speech since it seeks to influence people. It is sensitive to what people think and is a true Chameleon adapting its speech according to people. It corrupts advice and usurps authority which is not its own. It is a spirit who never repents, never apologizes, doesn't walk in love, a spirit who opposes God and fights the anointing of God.

The spirit of Jezebel seeks to influence and dominate the leaders, "the heads", because Jezebel wants to take their place and dominate in their place. Jezebel alone was responsible for the corruption of the nation of Israel; this is not a small spirit.

In the church, Jezebel proclaims herself a prophetess. She can disconnect the servants of God, to corrupt them in their thoughts, to fill them with lust for the things they do not have. It puts them out of service, and they become unusable by God. They become corrupted. They will not do anything for God. They will do things for themselves and not for God.

Indeed, Josette auto-proclaimed herself prophetess, many times, I heard her talking to people on the phone and predicted things by the spirit of divination. She held the bible and told them she was talking on behalf of God. I remember the day of our departure from Paris, where, certainly by the spirit of divination, she told me: "I'm going to get you settled and come back". But we shouldn't be troubled by the reality of this prophecy. The book of acts reveals that the Apostle Paul had delivered a servant girl who had a spirit of divination. She prophesied with the assistance of the spirit of python to earn money for her masters, though she was indeed stating real facts.

But glory be to God, the teaching in my notebook contained the solution: to overcome the spirit of Jezebel, one should practice two things, simplicity, and humility. This attitude may cause the person oppressed by this spirit to sanctify his heart.

We were a week away from our return to Paris, but I felt deep inside I should not go. I therefore said to Josette I would remain in Washington to monitor the projects I had assigned to partners and I would get to Paris later. She maintained her return date to October 10, 2008.

At home, our relationship with "Uncle Leo" had not changed. He was always as discreet and unobtrusive. Of course, he was not aware of the adventure between Josette and me. However, with Josette, the interactions were no longer the same as she wanted to exercise more authority over me. I was calm as I had already discerned the spirit animating her, and how, through prayer, I should overcome and destroy its plans against me. I prayed for it regularly and I have seen the results and the power of prayer. In my notes and lessons learned on the spirit of Jezebel, it is written when the spirit knows

Patricia Esther Secke

it has been unmasked, it attempts to the get rid or destroy by any means.

Two days before the departure of Josette, she gave me twenty-four hours to get out of the apartment of her cousin; without any explanation! I had to leave before her departure (I had paid for her round-trip ticket). In humility, I replied I was going to make my arrangements to leave the same day. I entered in my room, the heart in peace and with a calm attitude. I fastened my two suitcases and I was out. I had only one destination: The House of my father (the Church).

Once at church, I went to see Pastor Willy with whom I shared the news, and he told me: "all we have to do is pray". At the end of the service, Pastor Willy handed me his phone telling me Josette was on the line and wished to speak to me. "I picked up the call; it was Josette asking me to come back home quickly because she did not want to oppose God". Always calm and serene, I went back home.

No one can oppose the will of God, nor his decrees. I got home, I ate, and I went to bed. In the morning, on the day of her departure, she told me that God brought me to the United States for her cousin, to lead him to Christ since she believed that through me the light would shine in her family.

I replied I did not intend to remain in the United States or marry her cousin when I had a suitor waiting for me in Paris for marriage. She asked me to pray for her, I did sincerely. I presented her trip and her life to the hands of God, and she left the house at 10: 00 am for the airport.

CHAPITRE 10

THE REVELATION OF MY HUSBAND

CHAPITRE 10: THE REVELATION OF MY HUSBAND

As soon as she left, I felt a shift in the atmosphere of the apartment. As if a dense cloud had left the room. I opened all the doors of the apartment, I aerated, and said: Holy Spirit of God, come in this house and dwell here, bless this house. The next morning, when I woke up, I heard a voice which said to me: "Anoint the house with oil."

I got up and prayed while anointing the entire house with oil. All of this happened of course without "uncle" Léo knowing. I was unknowingly marking my territory once again, after declaring three weeks before I felt at home in his house. The next day, as usual, I listened to my sermon of the day on the internet. The spirit of God led me to listen to a message from Pastor Mohammed Sanogo in its entirety (May God bless him for the impact his message had on my life), which title was "leaving everything to possess". This was a special message which came expressly from heaven to radically change the course of my life and write an important page of my history.

This message built me up because pastor Sanogo dealt with the things preventing us from taking possession of our inheritance and blessings like Abram. When God asked Abram to leave, he took his entire family with him to fulfill the mission God had entrusted him: Genesis 12, verse 1 and 2 "Now the

LORD had said unto Abram, Get thee out of thy country, and from thy kindred, and from thy father's house, unto a land that I will shew thee: And I will make of thee a great nation, and I will bless thee, and make thy name great; and thou shalt be a blessing".

 The man of God said in his message that as long as Abram was not separated from his father Terach and his nephew Lot, he simply traveled throughout the Promised Land, but did not possess it. It is only when his father died and once, he separated himself from his nephew Lot that he was able to enter into the possession of his inheritance.

The message said we need to separate ourselves from "the Terach and Lot" of our lives to possess our inheritance and fulfill our destiny planned by God. "Terach and Lot" are obstacles and pitfalls which can either be an attitude, or a person, or a behavior hindering us from walking towards our destiny. It could be focusing on someone we deem essential to our lives or an absolute confidence in a plan or project we think can succeed on its own and by all means.

This teaching befuddled me and opened my eyes on my surroundings and my state of mind. The scales fell from my eyes and I saw clearly. I had a suitor for marriage in Paris who didn't conform to the type of husband I asked God, yet I was bound to think he could be my husband.

At the end of his message, Pastor Sanogo asked anyone whose heart was affected by this message and the word of God to repent and submit to the will of God. I humbled myself before the Lord, I repented for thinking my will was God's will. I pledged to separate myself from anything that could impede me from fulfilling my destiny and I submitted to God's perfect will. I said to God: "Lord, here I am such as I am before you, I renounce everything which is not of you in my life, I renounce to my own plans; Here I am in America, I don't know anyone, I don't know what I am doing in this country, do what you want of me, I abandon myself to you father. Amen!"

After this sincere prayer to God, I remained lying on the carpet for several minutes, silent, and then I heard this voice telling me: "my daughter you're here at home, here is the husband I have selected for you" what? I jumped on my two feet, what? "Uncle Leo?" my husband? I'm here in my home?

I didn't hear more, the Lord had established and fulfilled me. The man with the stature I wanted from the bottom of my heart had been reserved for me by God himself. God knows what is good for us. A week later, "Uncle Leo" told me he wanted me to be his wife. The word of God does not return to him

Patricia Esther Secke

void without having performed what it was sent for. May my marriage be to the honor and glory of God!

CHAPITRE 11
GOD OF FAVOR

CHAPITRE 11: GOD OF FAVOR

After God confirmed my final departure from France, I went back to Paris to pack my belongings and vacate my apartment. I had planned to permanently leave France on February 2, 2009. I got a one-way ticket at a good price in an English airline. It was a non-refundable and non-exchangeable ticket.

On the evening of February 1st, the weather forecast of France and Europe announced a snowstorm for February 2nd. At 5 a.m., I was ready, bags fastened, very confident to leave once and for all France. I had to be at the airport at 7:00 am in the morning the reason being that the take-off was scheduled for 9:00 am. My brother and longtime friend, Koffi which was to take me to the airport called at 5: 30 am to inform me that the snow was abundant in his neighborhood and his car slid on the snow. I called one of my associates who lived not far from me, and who was willing to drop me.

The snow had indeed covered several centimeters of the streets of Paris, but the major roads were plowed. Only, the traffic jams and traffic were significant, we got there within three hours and arrived at the airport at 9: 30 a.m. I feared the plane had left. I greeted and thanked my associate and I headed straight to the information desk. The flight that would take me to Washington, DC had not left.

The English airline had cancelled all its flights of the day due to the snow. Thank God! I still had a chance to travel since my delay had no consequence on my trip and because it is the company itself who had cancelled its flights. I went to the check-in desk of the airline; the line was long.

Some passengers were asked to come back two days later, others were simply asked to wait according to their destination. I prayed and asked for God to be gracious unto me and find me a flight on the same day for Washington, DC, because I didn't want to stay in Paris another day. I couldn't picture myself making the trip back with all the snow and then wait a couple of days to travel. When it was my turn, the hostess simply found me a seat on a flight on the same day for Washington, DC.

God can make a way in chaos, in an entanglement, in a situation of confusion to accomplish his word and his purposes. Despite the time which was not in my favor from a human standpoint, the disastrous weather condition, the postponement and cancellation of flights for several passengers, God showed me grace and gave me favor; I had to go. I had to leave France.

When I arrived in Washington, DC, my husband was already waiting for several hours. I could see the exhaustion, the joy and relief in his eyes. Once at home, by making a the toast in my honor, he said "welcome home" this sentence immediately reminded me the voice of the Holy Spirit I had heard four months before, and confirmed to me the words I had then heard when I prayed here "my daughter you are at home here, here is the husband I have selected for you".

It was also the day of my birthday. The house was decorated with nice words and balloons around us, I was happy as a little girl. I was happy. I knew Jesus had opened a door before me no one could shut. He had just put me on the real corridor of my destiny.

God showed me some key points in my mission requiring specific skills and tools adequate for some specific projects; I discovered with great pleasure and admiration, that the Lord who orchestrates all things had made my husband an honorable University Professor in the United States of America. Dr. Secke holds a doctorate of state in Finance and Banking from the University of Paris Sorbonne in France. After working as an Inspector and operations controller at the Cameroonian State Bank, the "Cameroon Bank", and disappointed by the light and frivolous management of the governmental financial institutions in Cameroon, he expatriated to the United States where he developed his skills at the service of education.

CHAPITRE 12

DO GOOD AND LEND TO OTHERS WITHOUT EXPECTING ANYTHING IN RETURN

Patricia Esther Secke

CHAPITRE 12: DO GOOD AND LEND TO OTHERS WITHOUT EXPECTING ANYTHING IN RETURN

Throughout this period of transition, the Lord continued to teach me, to mold me. He has worked extensively on my heart and continues to do so. Before leaving Paris, my aunt Calixte was staying with me in my apartment for about a year and a half, and she got saved by the grace of God, in the church I used to attend. I provided housing for aunt Calixte, and I never asked her any contribution for the rent, although she worked regularly and was receiving a monthly salary. On my first trip to Washington, I stayed there for almost three months, and my rent remained outstanding throughout this period, even though she was residing at home.

The landlord claimed his payments and Calixte in my absence, offered to pay the outstanding balance for the three months' rent, provided the landlord transferred the rental lease in her name. The landlord with whom I was in contact with since Washington, DC, declined her offer and informed me, I need to specify that Calixte lived in Paris for four years and could not find any housing.

God said "For there is nothing covered that shall not be revealed; neither hid, that shall not be known. Therefore, whatsoever ye have spoken in darkness shall be heard in the light; and that which ye have spoken in the ear in closets shall be proclaimed upon the housetops" Luke 12, verse 2 and 3.

While Calixte was doing all these negotiations without my knowledge, my Lord revealed to me in a dream the state of her soul: in the dream, she and I were walking and were concerned about a problem which concerned her solely, and that had to be resolved. I was taking her somewhere since I was the person who knew the path which led to her solution, and she followed me. To address this situation, we needed money, and I personally did not have money, and she told me she didn't have anything either. While she told me she had nothing, the Holy Spirit told me she had money, but did not want to use it. Though deep inside she wanted me to resolve the issue, and knew I had the solution for her.

The Lord said: "I will tell you great things, hidden things which you know not", in John 16 verse 13: "when the comforter is come, the spirit of truth… he will guide you into all the truth….and he will tell you things to come".

Upon my arrival in Paris, I was determined to return the apartment to the landlord, to release Calixte, and definitively leave France.

Our pastor in paris, Pastor Jean-Paul Munganga, who was aware of the housing predicament of my aunt (since it was a matter of prayer at church) and my decision to leave for the United States, called me and told me I held the solution to Calixte housing issue. I was the channel God chose to bless her, and for the love of Christ, I had to negotiate and plead with the landlord of that apartment on her behalf so that the apartment be rented to her and transferred in her name.

Certain things, humanly speaking are sometimes hard to do, especially for a person who has an evil heart and openly tries to take advantage of you. But the love of Christ in us causes us to go beyond our human nature, and love our enemies, our adversaries and those who throw a wrench into our endeavors.

The love of Christ banishes any hatred, resentment, and overcomes sin. The enemy seeks very often to keep us captives with grudges, animosities, personal vendettas, quarrels, mutterings, to blind us to the glory of God and steal our blessings. However, the blessings of the Lord are unlimited and are available to us. It is our sins and hardness of heart that prevent us from taking possession of them.

The ways of the Lord are extraordinary, and it is amazing to see the way he shapes us, molds us, and makes us vessels of honor. I had three months of unpaid rent, I had to face the landlord for the closure of my leasing record, and as if this were not enough, I had to increasingly argue for the issue of aunt Calixte and do everything for the transfer of lease.

I obeyed and went to see the landlord. When I had moved in the apartment ten years ago, I had paid a deposit corresponding to two months of rent. It was an amount which was to be reimbursed at the end of my lease. My outstanding rent was equal to three months rent; my account had a deficit amounting to one month's rent. Therefore, I had to pay to the agency about 610 euros to settle the balance on my account and terminate the rental agreement, on the date of the appraisal scheduled for the following week.

Once my record was closed, I pleaded for my aunt and I managed to convince the landlord who agreed to rent her the apartment. Her contract was to take effect on the day of my exit appraisal.

On that day, I only had 500 euros instead of 610 euros needed to pay the residue of my debt and settle the balance on my account. I was 110 euros short. The law required as I had done ten years previously the payment of two months of deposit to move in the apartment, and my aunt had prepared her money. To our pleasant surprise, the landlord informed us while the law had changed and that from now on, she must pay the amount of one month of deposit.

Patricia Esther Secke

My aunt paid immediately. I who had no more money on me was hoping that Calixte, out of gratefulness for my intervention on her behalf would be assisting me with the 110 euros out of her surplus. Unfortunately, she kept her money as I had seen in my dream a few weeks before. And as the Lord had revealed me her state of mind, I just thanked God for her. I gave him thanks for making me a channel of blessings. "The liberal soul shall be made fat: and he that watereth shall be watered also himself." Proverbs 11:25. God asks us to love your enemies, and do good, and lend, hoping for nothing again; and your reward shall be great, and ye shall be the children of the Highest: for he is kind unto the unthankful and to the evil. Luke 6 verse 35.

Two days later, I took my plane for America, but the trial with aunt Calixte was not over. A few months later, I had to stop in Paris on my way back from a trip. I didn't think about my lodging since I assumed, I would be staying with my aunt.

She had put the keys to the apartment at my disposal since she was on vacation. Once in the apartment, I soon understood there was a problem because the door of the bedroom was locked. I called her from a pay phone (since she had locked the phone in the bedroom) to ask her what was going on, she told me her girlfriend to whom she had entrusted the apartment in her absence had certainly locked the bedroom for security purposes. I recovered the keys with her girlfriend, and I was able to get in the bedroom. To my surprise, the phone had been unplugged from the phone jack and hidden. I could not call in the city neither have internet access, nor even receive calls.

I was astounded how could aunt Calixte do this to me? I who hosted her for over a year in the same apartment and I travelled regularly without ever locking the door of this same bedroom. The building was secure. In ten years, we never had a theft in this private residence. How was such behavior possible? I even remembered that at times, I slept in the living room for several months and I gave her my room and my bed. How could my aunt do this to me? I who did everything for her to have this apartment in her name? I who had left her my kitchenware, storage furniture how could she behave so with me?

I was deeply hurt within myself. I talked to a few people around me who advised me to empty the apartment of all my furniture; either give them away or put them in the trash seeing that Calixte's behavior was really distressing and unacceptable.

But this was not what my heart wanted me to do. The next day Sunday, I went to church. On my way, I was talking to God asking some explanations about the situation and I told him: "Lord, what are you going to tell me today that can comfort me and relieve my grief, what are you going to tell me for me not to pack all my furniture and give it away to other people?"

Once at the church, we had a guest pastor who came from London. He preached on brokenness!

The pastor preached particularly on the meaning of the work of Jesus on the cross of Golgotha, a work which comes down to love, the manifestation of God's love for men. He explained that agreeing to follow Jesus is to die to self, to renounce to pride, to the "me", it is going beyond this reasoning which leads us to say, "How can she do this to me?" "I who gave her this or that". As long as the evil deeds of the people around us lead us to revenge, it means we are not broken. We are not prepared for the ministry or mission whom God calls us to, and we are not worthy to follow Jesus.

The love for our neighbor must be expressed at all levels. Christ cannot be the head of a corrupt body, filled with hate and a desire for revenge. Christ is the head of a body that looks like him. Christ has never called for revenge, for accusation for being accused, to any kind of claim, since we are under a new Covenant in Christ: the covenant of grace and love. We must walk according to grace and love. We must manifest this love to our neighbor.

Divine love loves its enemy. Christ living in us causes us to love our persecutors. The disciple must be as the master, when we are offended, we must forgive and say like Jesus on the cross, who was betrayed, insulted, rejected: "father, forgive them for they do not know what they do". Jesus said to his disciples in Matthew 5 verses 43 to 45: "Ye have heard that it hath been said, thou shalt love thy neighbor, and hate thine enemy. But I say unto you, Love your enemies, bless them that curse you, do good to them that hate you, and pray for them which despitefully use you, and persecute you; That ye may be the children of your Father which is in heaven: for he maketh his sun to rise on the evil and on the good, and sendeth rain on the just and on the unjust".

Our God doesn't call for revenge since he said in Deuteronomy 32, verse 35 "To me belong revenge and retribution". Revenge doesn't belong to us, we must pray for those who have hurt us and the anger in us will disappear. If we are not able to love our enemies, then we are not sons of our father. Matthew 5 verse 4 "happy are they that mourn for they shall be comforted".

This powerful word of comfort led me to burst into tears for I realized I still had a long way to go in my consecration to the Lord Jesus. The senior pastor had planned for me to speak of my mission to the congregation. He invited me to speak, and to the surprise of the entire congregation, I did not talk about my mission. I simply shared about the experience I was going through and testified about the word I just received from the man of God. The Holy Spirit had just impacted my mentality and had taken me to a higher dimension in my relationship with Christ. I shared this experience with my aunt in the congregation, I prayed for aunty Calixte, and I asked the church to join me in prayer for her.

At the end of this trial, I realized that for God to use me there would be a price to pay. The only sacrifice befitting God is a broken and contrite spirit for power cannot be released to babies. We can only be victorious after we have endured and overcome the hindrances. When we endure obstacles, we can use our experience, to help others overcome hindrances.

Proper preparation always precedes the blessings, and preparation is made in our daily activities. I am in the school of the Holy Spirit. God teaches us to get along with all sorts of people by surrounding us with people who exasperate us and make us crazy. We must not run away from them, otherwise, we will find worse where we will go. These frustrations are nutrients for our spiritual growth. We are not ready for what God has planned for us if we are offended in our hearts. God prepares us in sanctification. I bless aunty Calixte that God used to make me grow in my consecration.

Chapter 13

My MISSION

NO ONE CAN DESTROY A WORK OR A MANDATE FROM GOD

Chapter 13: My MISSION

NO ONE CAN DESTROY A WORK OR A MANDATE FROM GOD

In February 2009, I had completely moved to the United States, and I was preparing for the 3rd International Congress of Black Women to be held in November 2009 in Kinshasa in the Democratic Republic of Congo, under the patronage of the first lady. I had set up a team of ten people in charge of the preparations of this major event. It was the first Congress in Africa; the challenges were therefore very important.

In July 2009, my team and I had made a first trip to Kinshasa to fine tune the final preparations. In the group there was Vicki who was in charge of preparing the delegation from France attending the Conference. In addition to this task, she had integrated the public relations team during the organizational trip. This group of Public Relations was also in charge of the search for sponsors in Kinshasa. But Vicki was doing business behind the back of the organization; entering one door of negotiations and coming out from another without giving us the time to figure out what she was doing.

During an appointment with the head of one major company of telephony in Congo, who had already agreed to sponsor us, Vicki during the closing of the contract ushered in her husband in the meeting room, who immediately pleaded for his bid which had been pending with the company for a long time. There was a general malaise in the meeting room. The executive took leave of us and we never received any sponsorship from this company.

All the trips we've made so far have been at our expense; no state, no government paid for our tickets when we were travelling around to talk about powerful women's vision. Vicki took the liberty to request a reimbursement for our airline tickets (it was mostly for her own) to the Director of the cabinet of the first lady; which was an unprofessional move.

I had to refocus our objectives by stating that we did not come to the Congo to request a reimbursement for our expenses, but to work and show that women of the African Diaspora can lead concrete projects with success and in the long term in Africa. I also apologized to the Director of the Cabinet for the unprofessional behavior of my associate. It was already many missteps in a short time.

A few days later, we were in late July 2009, and had ended the first part of our mission. We were going back to our respective countries, as some came from France, South Africa, Cameroon and Washington.

We had to come back three weeks before the beginning of the Congress scheduled for November 28, 2009.

In September, I heard persistent rumors coming from Paris saying the Congress would not take place. The people who were telling me that claimed the information came from Vicki. Indeed, it had been two months since I had heard from the office of the first lady, and curiously no one answered my phone calls to Congo any longer, or even my emails. The team started to pray. I only had God, I prayed and reminded God he was the one who told me in 2007, when my feet trampled the Congolese soil: "you are at the heart of Africa; it is here that I want you to do the first Congress in Africa, because it is the heart of Africa".

After my prayers, I felt a peace, and with confidence, I pursued my work with the women of the African Diaspora in America and Europe.

Adele, a Congolese in the European Diaspora, attended as guest of honor the first two conferences which took place in Paris in 2007 and 2008. Adele laid claim to the Congress taking place in the Congo. She was one of the first people who had asked the first lady of the Congo to accept to sponsor the event. I remember back in February 2008, Adele called me in Kinshasa to let me know she had arranged an appointment with the first lady, and I absolutely needed to get to Kinshasa. I had no money, so two friends lent me money and I left. Upon my arrival, Adele told me: "I met the first lady yesterday, and she agreed to sponsor the Congress".

She made me come to the Congo to meet the first lady of the country, and then informed me once I arrived, she had already met her without me! Without making a fuss about it, I began to work. I organized a press conference to share the vision and to educate Congolese women on the importance of this Conference for their business and their country.

I never saw the first lady on this occasion in 2008. I was not particularly anxious to see her on that occasion for I knew God had a plan, and he knew how to orchestrate things.

Towards the end of the month of September, I received an email from the Congo, an anonymous person who God used blind copied me on Adele and her sister Raïssa emails who plotted to discredit me in the eyes of the Congolese Government and to make the Conference fail. They were determined to bring me down.

The rumor in Paris was more prevalent and several people confirmed that Adele had the power to make this Conference fail considering she had great connections and could influence the Congolese Government. I replied to them that my greatest connection is Jesus; He who charged me to organize the Congress in the Congo. With hindsight, I think these people I talked with viewed me as naïve and really believed everything was over for me. I myself simply stood on God's instruction to organize the first Congress in 2009 in the Congo, and I was seriously preparing without considering the circumstances and oppositions.

Patricia Esther Secke

On October 03, 2009, my team and I landed in Kinshasa after fasting and praying. Vicki was no longer part of the team, but she went on with her campaign of intoxication, and destabilization, which did not make me worried.

We prayed for the favor of God and asked him to change the spiritual atmosphere in Kinshasa as soon as we would set foot on the Congolese soil. Like the example of the 4 lepers who arrived in the Syrian camp and silenced the entire army that had risen up against the people of God (2 King 7).

Adele and Vicki were the main instigators of the conspiracy against the 3rd Conference in Kinshasa. Upon our arrival, a member of the Government warned me about their scheme to make us fail and showed me a copy of their correspondence with the head of state, in which they requested the cancellation of the Congress because a Cameroonian was coming to swindle and deceive Congolese women. Her letter also suggested to the first lady to preclude me and take the project away from me so that the Congolese would be in charge. I must specify that Adele is a Belgian citizen, but of Congolese origin. She took advantage of her position in the Belgian Government to influence the decision of the Congolese Government.

I read this correspondence very carefully, and I simply responded to the member of the Government that if this work is of men, men will make it fail, but if it is of God, no one can destroy it. May the instigators of a potential failure not run the risk of having fought against God! When the mandate comes from God, no one can destroy it. Acts 5, verses 38 and 39.

The Congolese Government, particularly the women in charge of this project had taken into account the letter of Adele, and Vicki's many calls to the Presidential offices, and chose to handle the situation in their own way by denying our Organization the use of the amount of more than 500000 dollars allocated by the President of the Republic to support this meeting, which would put forward the work of Congolese women and the achievements made by black women in the world.

The Government officials in charge of the management of these funds, decided deliberately not to put the operational budget at our disposal on the ground. Moreover they requested us to pay for some major expenses for the Congress such as the airfare for more than 40 people, the speakers, the trainers and the guests of honor, their lodging, food for ten days, as well as meals during the Congress for one thousand people for 2 days, the charges for the hostesses, the brochures for all participants and other services related to the Congress, without counting the support of our international team of about ten people.

Patricia Esther Secke

We were promoter of the event in the world. We worked day and night for the success of this global meeting, and for the Democratic Republic of Congo, which until then was known on the international level as a country with rampant wars, rape of women, misery, poverty, AIDS, to be seen in other light by the world and the international media as a country where it is good to live and where the potential of women is significant for its contribution in the development of the country, and the African continent.

We have suffered oppression after oppression, threats, and intimidation. A Lady from the Government, a friend of Vicki's who was in charge of the lodging of our team which arrived in the DRC three weeks before the Congress (four people from Washington and Paris) never paid for the hotel expenses. We had one evening, during the organization of the Congress, to sleep on the carpet in one room as the other rooms were locked for non-payment. We stayed a month in the Congo and had to cover ourselves the expenses for our lodging, food, transportation, gas, phone, airplane tickets, etc. Our efforts resulted in a Congress with over five thousand attendees, eminent personalities from abroad and high-level trainers who came to support and honor the Congolese women.

But glory be to God for his faithfulness as participants registration fees and the financial support of four sponsors enabled us to pay off more than half of our bills. God was at work and he honored us. We had a lot of opposition, battles at all levels, especially with members of the Government, and mainly women.

THE CONDUCTING OF THE CONGRESS

As soon as we were in Kinshasa, with our team in place, we worked strategically to educate women. Despite the pressures, things were being organized in an amazing way, and women were coming from all over. They wanted to understand what was being prepared. They wanted to get involved. They wanted to make their contribution; they wanted to show what they can do. They wanted to express themselves.

Apart from the denial from the members of the government in charge of the budget, to cooperate with us for the sharing of the expenses, there was a remarkable mobilization at the level of the government. On the day of the Congress, all the institutions of the government, the diplomatic corps, and women of all social strata were present.

Our trainers have trained approximately one thousand women on business management, the African renaissance, business networking, the power of network, the power of the unity of women vital for the development of Africa.

We had the honor in this Congress, to welcome the first ladies of the Democratic Republic of Congo, the Republic of Zambia and the Republic of Congo Brazzaville. They availed themselves, participated in the plenary sessions, made the round of the market square and interacted with the attendees.

Market square is a concept we have put in place to provide visibility and recognition to women who are in the shadows but are leading concrete and targeted actions on the ground. To help them come out of the isolation, the anonymity and share their talents with other women by creating adequate connections.

The President of the Democratic Republic of the Congo, his Excellency Mr. Joseph Kabila, has also honored us with his presence at the Gala of the Palms for the Excellence of Women which was the closing event. A panel of successful women of our organization was awarded trophies, as a symbol of recognition for their bravery and professionalism in their sector of activity.

Immediately after the Congress, we left the Democratic Republic of Congo. We had succeeded and God moved in our favor. It was what mattered the most to me. Those who were conspiring to sabotage the Congress failed.

But they did not stop there seeing that when the devil can't destroy you, he plots defamation and accuses you; he is the accuser! But Jesus Christ precipitated the accuser. The award I received for the work accomplished by my team was: insults, name-calling, critics, and charges of any kind. A mail also circulated on the internet stating I had received a sum of three hundred thousand Euros from the first lady of the Congo. A few members of my team doubted me. They thought I had received money from the Congolese Government without giving them "their share". The most impatient and opportunistic members of my team did some business on the side and took envelopes from some Ministers. The frustrated ones abandoned the mission; the same people who claimed to have the deep conviction this work was truly of God and who had sworn to follow me everywhere.

The most troubling was that even some pastors, servants of God we brought along from Europe and America did not understand the role they had to play in this event where God was establishing the foundations for a breakthrough for Africa and the Congo. They had been blinded, seduced by the rumor on the money, they also reviled me, rejected me, instead of praying for me and praying against recurring injustice in Africa. Some have even thought I received money from the first lady. I understand many are not worthy to be with me, or rather to go on with me on this sacred mission. They allowed themselves to be overtaken by Mammon (God of money).

Patricia Esther Secke

Those who cannot or do not want to follow the ever-increasing spiritual rise of my work should not prevent its ascent. Jesus said: "We recognize them at their fruits". Their mouth speaks of God, and their hearts are filled with covetousness.

I resolved that in order to achieve my goals, I had to separate myself from those who weaken me. Otherwise they would lead me to failure and in hell.

I realized at the end of the 3rd Congress, when we do good things, many are there to take advantage. We work day and night, we do a remarkable job, but they pretend not to see anything, and when we are in a predicament, very few people are there to support us. I would like to thank Ms. Aurelia Mendes Talamaku, who has supported us tremendously at this Congress. May God remember the generous things she did for us!

God allowed these trials to test my ability to remain firmly attached to him and humble. The opposition I faced was a test to evaluate the level of confidence I had in what God had revealed to me.

My goal going to the Democratic Republic of Congo was not to make money, as everyone else thought; my goal was to obey God who instructed me to start the first Congress in Africa in this country. When leaving the country on the plane, I simply said: Lord, I did what you told me to, I acknowledge this was possible only because you willed it. I commit to you all the people who persecuted us, those who usurped what belonged to our organization, and I'm at peace because I have your promise which says "if the thief be found, let him pay double" Exodus 22 verse 7.

I know the word of God does not return to him without effect. God bless the Democratic Republic of Congo, for the perfect plan He has for this people.

Patricia Esther Secke

Chapter 14

RECEIVE MY INSTRUCTION, AND NOT SILVER; AND KNOWLEDGE RATHER THAN CHOICE GOLD. Proverbs 8 verse 10

Chapter 14: RECEIVE MY INSTRUCTION, AND NOT SILVER; AND KNOWLEDGE RATHER THAN CHOICE GOLD. Proverbs 8 verse 10

At the conclusion of the 3rd Congress, the first lady of Zambia wished to host the 4th Congress in her country to allow the Zambian women to benefit from the vision of our organization and its benefits. The African woman being at the heart of our mission, we agreed to discover the Zambian woman and together build an Africa that wins. We put ourselves to work for the 4th Congress in Zambia to be a success.

In January 2010, the first lady of Zambia came to the United States and personally called me to tell me she wanted us to start preparing early for a complete success. She sent me her email address and three months later, I received an official invitation from her asking me to make an organizational trip to Zambia in July. I went there with my associate Madam Parker Mabry. The trip was at the expense of the organization: plane tickets, hotel and food.

The first lady hosted a breakfast in our honor, where Zambian companies were present. She solemnly announced the holding of the next Congress and had set up an organizational committee that would work closely with our organization Africa Femmes Performantes.

Patricia Esther Secke

Two months before the holding of the Congress in Zambia in early November 2010, the Zambian organizational committee announced to me the United Nations, through their body working to eradicate poverty in poor countries by 2015 (UNDP: United Nations development program) wanted to be a partner of the 4th Congress and sponsor around one hundred thousand dollars. The idea seemed interesting. We had a conference call with the Committee of the first lady and the officers of the UNDP in Zambia.

They wanted to change the concept of Africa Femmes Performantes and replace it with the program of the United Nations development program. In 2000, the United Nations set its Millennium targets for the development by planning to eradicate poverty by 2015 in all poor countries of the world, particularly in Africa. We were already in 2010; their eradication program had not really progressed. The opportunity with our activities in Zambia was a justification parade.

The Officers of the UNDP in Zambia came to find in Africa Femmes Performantes a good alibi to justify they were doing some work. They sent me by email a program of 7 pages in which the vision God had given did not appear anymore. They changed the title of our event, the concept became: "The UNDP *organizes in partnership with Africa Femmes*

Performantes the 4ᵗʰ Congress of the African woman" the whole program we had worked on for over a year petered out, for one hundred thousand dollars.

This reminded me an interesting sermon which said the birthing of a vision and/or a child is always a fight. The closer we get to this real child, the closer the devil gets to us trying to devour him. If the devil cannot prevent us from establishing our vision, the first strategy he will use to destroy us, is to try to be involved in the mission, try to help us. But this help is a disaster. What profited a man to win the whole world and lose his soul?

The one hundred thousand dollars offer from the United Nations to sponsor the Congress was a bait to attract us to their nets and subsequently destroy us. It would prove that Africans cannot organize anything on their own and should always be assisted by international organizations. Poverty is the supporting evidence of the existence of UNDP in Africa. Once an African organization begins to work seriously with palpable results, they will no longer have any reason to be and remain in Africa. Therefore, they must destroy beneath the surface any organization designed to empower African, first by helping and then by hijacking the concept.

I replied flatly "no" to this suggestion since I knew that these one hundred thousand dollars would not be used for the promotion of women in Zambia. UNDP was in Zambia to eradicate poverty, and it did not need to partner with us to do their job. Additionally, the Committee of the first lady wanted to put this money in an account managed by them and asked for the contribution of our organization to be put in the same account without us having the signature authorization.

Zambia is ranked as one of the poorest countries of the world. A woman wishing to start a small business in the market needs 50 dollars as capital, or 250000 Kwasha (Zambian franc). Why the UNDP, which certainly holds analyses and reports on the working situation of women in Zambia, doesn't directly work with women locally to impact and promote their work? One hundred thousand dollars would considerably advance the goals of the Millennium for development in Zambia without partnering with Africa Femmes Performantes.

The organizational committee did not digest my refusal and decided to prevent the holding of the 4th International Congress of Black Women in Zambia.

We were subjects to defamation, and sabotage. The head of communication of the first lady in connivance with the new Ambassador of Zambia to Washington, DC made a report to the first lady via its organizational committee stating that we were not listed in any US official records, and the first lady should not get involved with this type of organization, which would discredit the image of the First Lady of Zambia. The same Ambassador sent me an email recommending me to accept the offer of the UNDP since it was the only condition required by the first lady to be involved in this project. I refused this offer.

The Zambian Government cancelled the Congress for one hundred thousand dollars. God having the solution to any situation allowed us to bounce back and organize the Congress in Cameroon. The participants followed the movement, in Cameroon; we had 10 days of rehabilitation, a total delegation of 150 people coming from abroad and a successful 4th Congress with more than 500 people total.

Our sponsors followed us, it was an outstanding Congress, which allowed these women to understand the challenges and adversities we face in Africa for a real development and a total freedom from slavery, from the yoke of the Western powers and our enemy which is ourselves. Africans must learn to deal with Africans for Africa to step back from the brink. God admonishes us to prefer instructions to money, and that's what I did. God kept us from shame, failure, and catastrophe. All these tests are solid food preparing us for greater success.

Patricia Esther Secke

Chapter 15

THE FAITHFULNESS OF GOD

Chapter 15: THE FAITHFULNESS OF GOD

Our Lord is calling us for his own purposes. He is faithful and he orchestrates all things. The Lord revealed to me the goal of this mission was the restoration of all the black people who experienced four centuries of slavery since the 14th century, the sharing of its land due to an arbitrary division in 1885 at the Berlin Conference, colonization, imperialism, scorn, humiliation. The black people even today, at the dawn of the third millennium, suffer atrocities and injustices which go beyond human comprehension. The slavery of blacks never ended; it simply took another form over time.

When God reveals himself to us, he always confirms his will in the Holy Scriptures. The prophetic mandate of my mission is found in Isaiah 43 verse 5-7: "Fear not: for I am with thee: I will bring thy seed from the east, and gather thee from the west; I will say to the north, Give up; and to the south, Keep not back: bring my sons from far, and my daughters from the ends of the earth; Even every one that is called by my name: for I have created him for my glory, I have formed him; yea, I have made him".

When I understood my mission, I did not know what direction to take and what strategy to adopt. I have learned to trust the Lord regarding work strategies and for the mobilization of contact and key people to move with me for the fulfillment and realization of this mission.

Patricia Esther Secke

A door is open with African American women in whom God put the desire to return to Africa, those whom he called himself; in order to work for Africa and to work towards a real start. "It is the Lord himself who chooses us, who positions each person according to his glorious purposes: Ye have not chosen me, but I have chosen you, and ordained you, that ye should go and bring forth fruit, and that your fruit should remain" John 15 verse 16.

God is true. His plans for the African people will come to pass. Africa will experience freedom. Black people will be restored in an amazing way as predicted by the prophets of the Lord! The price our ancestors paid by their resistance and their blood, and the price Jesus Christ himself paid on the cross through every drop of his bloodshed for the total deliverance of his people, have not flowed in vain. There is a time for everything; God remembered the black race and decided to justify it.

I praise the Lord Jesus Christ, who called us in his harvest. I praise him for his workers that he selected for his harvest. He is faithful and he will do it. 1 Thessalonians 5: 24.

CONCLUSION

Patricia Esther Secke

CONCLUSION

The words I have on my heart as I am writing this conclusion are words of exhortation and encouragement.

Since my conversion to Christ, I had a lot of trials in the process of birthing the vision God had given me. Yet I kept my confidence in God, even in the most difficult times I remembered what God has done for me, his goodness in my life. He gave me the comfort he judged good for me so that I am enabled to fulfill my potential and serve him.

He gave me an understanding husband, pleasant to live with, he gave me a haven of peace. Jesus is the prince of peace, and since I chose to walk with him, I am in peace, inexplicable peace. Though certain things caused me to act precipitously in the past, today, I know how to be patient and wait for God's timing.

Intimidations in a crisis or in a confusing situation no longer make me panic because I walk by faith. I know when the devil insists in his strategies of oppression and intimidation; the victory will ensue after holding firm. I know God is in control of everything and his light always breaks forth according to his purposes and not according to my designs.

The mission God has entrusted to me requires considerable financial means. When I'm in an impasse, I remember a miracle God had done in my favor in 2008. We were a month away from the 2nd Congress, and I did not have enough funds to complete the organization of the event. I was invited to a fundraising gala organized by the first lady of Congo Brazzaville in Paris. I didn't know anyone there outside of Amelia who had invited me. We were on a table of 8 people all millionaires.

And there I was in the middle, wondering what I was doing there. The Fundraising ceremony began, and the millionaires were making donations by announcing the amount of their donations. I was drowned in this atmosphere of money floating around. Moreover, I had the stress of the Congress which was approaching fast while I did not have the enough provision for its preparation.

This time I asked God "Lord, what am I doing here?" "There is so much money floating around, and I don't have enough funds to finalize the preparation for the next Congress", then I heard this soft voice tell me: "the word of God is the solution to all your problems". When it is meditated, pressed with faith, it produces an anointing which operates miracles as the word of God cannot return to God without fulfilling its purpose on Earth.

Patricia Esther Secke

Immediately, a verse of the bible came to mind, it is the word that suited the situation: Isaiah 45:14: "thus says the Lord The labor of Egypt and merchandise of Ethiopia (symbol of the world and of the unbelievers)... shall come over unto thee, and they shall be thine".

I had my miracle in my hand. I immediately began to proclaim quietly this word, to pray for God's grace and favor. My mind was interceding, I was pressing the word, and I pressed with faith, suddenly, the head of the company TRAFIGURA, (a large oil company) who was sitting opposite to me threw a joke on women.

Amelia was just on my right retorted by saying "be careful about what you say because you don't know who seating in front of you is, he said who is she" She is the President of the international Congress of black women. "Ah good?" and he spoke to me saying "tell me a bit about what you're doing".

I confirmed to him that I am the President of an organization promoting the talents of black women in the world, each year I organize congresses of women and the next one was going to be held in a month in Paris. Being seated next to his Swiss banker, he tapped him on the shoulder saying: "but this is the kind of event we must help and subsidize". "The foundation of our company can do it", and he asked me, "How much do you need"?

Intimidated since I didn't know him, and embarrassed to give an amount without consulting Amelia who had invited me, I came back to a human reasoning and forgot I had to release the anointing for miracles.

I wanted to look at Amelia and he told me, "no don't look at her, tell me how much you want for your Congress", I said nothing, he told his banker, "send her a grant next week for her Congress" his banker handed me his business card by telling me "send me your banking information on Monday and I will send you 15 000 dollars". A week later, I had the 15 000 dollars in the organization's account.

God is true. God is faithful and wants to help us. God is a God of miracles who watches over His word to perform it, let us learn to trust him. I urge you to use the Holy Scriptures as your inspiration in everything you do.

You can like me accomplish your goals and deepest dreams, provided you submit to God's Word. Obeying God' precepts, is having the authority to do the greater works Jesus Christ had released. No matter the hardships, traps, conspiracies, plots against you or your projects, stand firm and put your trust in the Lord, because those who trust in the Lord shall renew their strength. They shall fly as eagles.

Patricia Esther Secke

They shall run, and not grow weary, walk, and not faint. The victory is inevitable at the end.

God bless you.